Animals That Live in the Desert/
Animales del desierto

Coyotes/Coyotes

By JoAnn Early Macken

Reading Consultant: Jeanne Clidas, Ph.D.
Director, Roberts Wesleyan College Literacy Clinic

Gareth Stevens
PUBLISHING

Please visit our website, www.garethstevens.com. For a free color catalog of all our high-quality books, call toll free 1-800-542-2595 or fax 1-877-542-2596.

Library of Congress Cataloging-in-Publication Data

Macken, JoAnn Early, 1953–
[Coyotes. Spanish & English]
Coyotes = Coyotes / by JoAnn Early Macken.
p. cm. — (animals that live in the desert = Animales del desierto)
Includes bibliographical references and index.
ISBN-10: 1-4339-2060-3 ISBN-13: 978-1-4339-2060-8 (lib. bdg.)
ISBN-10: 1-4339-2456-0 ISBN-13: 978-1-4339-2456-9 (soft cover)
1. Coyote—Juvenile literature. I. Title.
QL737.C22M3418 2010
599.77'25—dc22 2009009779

This edition first published in 2010 by
Gareth Stevens Publishing
111 East 14th Street, Suite 349
New York, NY 10003

Executive Managing Editor: Lisa M. Herrington
Senior Editor: Barbara Bakowski
Cover Designers: Jennifer Ryder-Talbot and Studio Montage
Production: Studio Montage
Translators: Tatiana Acosta and Guillermo Gutiérrez
Library Consultant: Carl Harvey, Library Media Specialist, Noblesville, Indiana

Photo credits: Cover, pp. 7, 9 Shutterstock; pp. 1, 21 © Charlie Heidecker/Visuals Unlimited; p. 5 © Barbara Gerlach/Visuals Unlimited; pp. 11, 15 © Steven Holt/Stockpix.com; p. 13 © Elizabeth Delaney/Visuals Unlimited; p. 17 © Richard Day/Daybreak Imagery; p. 19 © Michael H. Francis

Printed in the United States of America

1 2 3 4 5 6 7 8 9 14 13 12 11 10 09

Table of Contents

Contenido

Boldface words appear in the glossary./
Las palabras en **negrita** aparecen en el glosario.

Wild Dogs

A coyote (kigh-OH-tee) is a wild dog. Coyotes are bigger than foxes. Coyotes are smaller than wolves.

Cánidos salvajes

El coyote es un cánido salvaje. Los coyotes son más grandes que los zorros. Los coyotes son más pequeños que los lobos.

Most coyotes are gray or brown. Coyotes that live in the **desert** have light-colored fur. The light color helps the coyotes stay cool.

La mayoría de los coyotes son grises o de color café. Los coyotes que viven en el **desierto** tienen el pelaje de color claro. El color claro los ayuda a soportar el calor.

Coyotes have bushy tails and long legs.
They can run fast.

Los coyotes tienen la cola muy peluda y las patas largas. Pueden correr muy deprisa.

tail/
cola

Coyotes have large, pointed ears. They hear well. They can hear other animals moving.

Los coyotes tienen las orejas grandes y puntiagudas. Tienen muy buen oído. Pueden oír el movimiento de otros animales.

ears/
orejas

Coyote Pups

Baby coyotes are called **pups**. Their mother feeds them milk at first.

Crías de coyote

A las crías de coyote las llamamos **cachorros**. Al principio, su madre las alimenta con leche.

pups/
cachorros

The pups live in a **den** for about two months. Their father guards the den. When the pups come out, he teaches them to hunt.

Los cachorros viven en una **madriguera** por unos dos meses. El padre vigila la madriguera. Cuando los cachorros salen, los enseña a cazar.

den/
madriguera

Coyote pups like to play. They leap and **pounce**. They paw each other's faces.

Los cachorros son muy juguetones. Brincan, se **abalanzan** unos sobre otros, y se lanzan manotazos.

Noisy Desert Hunters

Coyotes hunt **prey**, such as rabbits, mice, and snakes. They hunt at night, when the desert is cool. Coyotes also eat nuts and fruit.

Escandalosos cazadores del desierto

Los coyotes cazan **presas** como conejos, ratones y serpientes. Cazan de noche, cuando refresca en el desierto. Los coyotes también comen nueces y fruta.

prey (snake)/
presa (serpiente)

Coyotes are noisy! They howl and bark. They **yip** and yelp. They call across the desert.

¡Los coyotes son muy ruidosos! Aúllan y ladran. **Gimen** y gruñen. Su llamada atraviesa el desierto.

Fast Facts/Datos básicos

Height/ Altura	about 2 feet (61 centimeters) at the shoulder/ unos 2 pies (61 centímetros) en la cruz
Length/ Longitud	about 4 feet (1 meter) nose to tail/ unos 4 pies (1 metro) de nariz a cola
Weight/ Peso	about 45 pounds (20 kilograms)/ unas 45 libras (20 kilogramos)
Diet/ Dieta	small animals, fish, snakes, lizards, fruit, and nuts/ animales pequeños, peces, serpientes, lagartos, fruta y nueces
Average life span/ Promedio de vida	up to 14 years/ hasta 14 años

Glossary/Glosario

den: a place where wild animals rest or live

desert: a dry area with little rainfall

pounce: to jump on

prey: animals that are killed for food

pups: baby coyotes

yip: bark in a high-pitched tone

---

abalanzarse: saltar sobre algo

cachorros: crías de coyote y otros animales

desierto: zona seca donde cae poca lluvia

gemir: aullar con un tono muy agudo

madriguera: lugar donde descansa o vive un animal salvaje

presas: animales devorados por otros animales

For More Information/Más información

Books/Libros

Coyotes Are Night Animals/Los coyotes son animales nocturnos. Night Animals (series). Joanne Mattern. (Gareth Stevens, 2007)

What Desert Animals Eat/¿Qué comen los animales del desierto? Nature's Food Chains (series). Joanne Mattern (Gareth Stevens, 2006)

Web Sites/Páginas web

Coyote/Coyote

www.nhptv.org/natureworks/coyote.htm

See photos and learn more about this wild dog./Vean fotografías de estos cánidos salvajes y conozcan más datos sobre ellos.

Creature Feature: Coyotes/*Creature Feature*: Coyotes

kids.nationalgeographic.com/Animals/CreatureFeature/Coyote

Watch a video of pups playing, and listen to coyote sounds./ Miren un video de cachorros jugando y oigan los ruidos que hacen los coyotes.

Publisher's note to educators and parents: Our editors have carefully reviewed these web sites to ensure that they are suitable for children. Many web sites change frequently, however, and we cannot guarantee that a site's future contents will continue to meet our high standards of quality and educational value. Be advised that children should be closely supervised whenever they access the Internet.

Nota de la editorial a los padres y educadores: Nuestros editores han revisado con cuidado las páginas web para asegurarse de que son apropiadas para niños. Sin embargo, muchas páginas web cambian con frecuencia, y no podemos garantizar que sus contenidos futuros sigan conservando nuestros elevados estándares de calidad y de interés educativo. Tengan en cuenta que los niños deben ser supervisados atentamente siempre que accedan a Internet.

Index/Índice

About the Author

JoAnn Early Macken is the author of two rhyming picture books, *Sing-Along Song* and *Cats on Judy*, and more than 80 nonfiction books for children. Her poems have appeared in several children's magazines. She lives in Wisconsin with her husband and their two sons.

Información sobre la autora

JoAnn Early Macken ha escrito dos libros de rimas con ilustraciones, *Sing-Along Song* y *Cats on Judy*, y más de ochenta libros de no ficción para niños. Sus poemas han sido publicados en varias revistas infantiles. Vive en Wisconsin con su esposo y sus dos hijos.